MY SILENT LOUD

BY

DR. MALIK MUHAMMAD, PH.D.

MY SILENT LOUD © 2019 by Malik Muhammad

ISBN: 978-0-578-53166-3

First Book Edition 2019

Edited by Janie Franz, The Book Whisperer

Cover Art © 2019 by The Artist, Salaam Muhammad

www.mysilentloud.com

DEDICATION

To the younger me…

I dreamt of being me and it came true.

*What **THEY** say about you will **NEVER** be as*

*important as what **YOU** choose to believe.*

Make sure your voice inside is always the loudest.

CONTENTS

INTRODUCTION

This book is written with the intent to give a voice to all Black boys growing up like I did who felt they never could express with words the emotions and thoughts they were having every day. I hope to give to them a feeling of confidence that I wish I had at a younger age. It wasn't until I was taught to have a voice and learned how to validate my own journey that I started enjoying life and setting goals. This book is just me trying to ease the journey for those young, awkward, scared, and insecure Black boys so they don't have to endure the pain I did silently. Instead, they will start to talk loud to those who love them about what they are feeling so they can learn to overcome those obstacles and stop feeling invisible in this world.

6 INCHES VERSUS 6 FEET

Some people drown in 6 Inches of water and some in 6 feet. Sometimes I find myself listening to friends' problems and am in amazement at what they consider overwhelming versus what I consider overwhelming. I listen to people who have homes and nice cars complain about bills that are due or a check engine light as if their world is coming to an end while they pass older people in a 100-degree heat, waiting at a bus stop. It makes me wonder how we as people grow and learn to interpret our problems. It also makes me irritated because it feels like noise (static).

I see SO many people pass over or kick aside their blessings and choose to worry to create barriers to prevent them from doing the work required to accomplish a goal. Sometimes I think people prefer to complain rather than work. But what's the gain? I get irritated hearing the same complaints over and over with no movements to change.

A close friend told me "Either you bring those around you up or they will bring you down." So, I've worked on watching what or who I allow to take my energy. My energy is limited so I have the right and responsibility to gauge what and who I give it to. But when you are around anyone who's drowning in 6 inches of water right in front of you, then you have to always ask yourself if you are going to drown with them. Take time to point out to them that they are TRYING (choosing) to drown in a puddle or focus on what will keep YOU from getting wet.

A LIFE WITH BUILT-IN EXCUSES

The White man won't let me...

This is a phrase or a version of a phrase I have heard all my entire life. And let me be clear I have heard it from the richest to the poorest of my community. It still saddens me because it's just not true. White people do not... Let me repeat. WHITE PEOPLE DO NOT have the ultimate power over the outcomes in your life. YOU DO!! So many African Americans surrender their dreams and life goals before they even get started based on the fallacy that White people will stop them.

Based on my life, I haven't seen White people be overly concerned about what I'm doing. That is not to say racism and prejudice don't create hurdles and barriers.

But let me ask you this: You, the reader, do you think every dream a White person has comes true? Are they all CEOs? Doctors? Lawyers? Do these White people who do not succeed blame "the White man" or any other man? No. They should blame themselves!! Just like any African American who blames the ghost of White consciousness for their own failures.

To me this way of thinking has created a life with built-in excuses for African Americans to not try, not dream. The hardest thing for anyone to do it to try. Especially, to try without any guarantee of success. And then to try again after failing.

I know I've had to go after my goals without a plan. And I look back and remember someone telling me "You made getting a PhD look easy." This surrendering statement still gives me pause. By no means was getting my doctorate easy! I think what "made it look easy" was that I never let the process I was experiencing take away my laughter for long periods of time.

When I was young, I studied at the Carl Rogers Institute for Studies of the Person. There I really learned what it means to live in the moment. When I practice living in the moment, it greatly reduces and sometime even can eliminate worries about the future. By trying to live this way (especially in stressful times), I've been able to be more relaxed than others at times that are pure panic for them. So it's not that my life has or is easy. It's that I always pursue ways to interpret my journey in a way that allows me to have hope.

For African Americans that believe a mysterious White man is walking behind them and robbing them of success, I believe they themselves are the thieves robbing them of their dreams. I can't believe that a people who came from some of the strongest to ever live on planet Earth cannot thrive and succeed when they put their minds to it.

I'm not disappointed in my people. I just said for my ancestors, they deserve a better celebration for their struggles. My ancestors literally lived so that some day, century away from them, a knucklehead like me would be called Doctor. Is it not the least I can do with each of my breaths to strive for greatness instead of surrendering my power to some imaginary White man in my imagination?

A WARRIOR IN ENEMY TERRITORY

B eing a young Black man growing up in America is like being a Warrior growing up in enemy territory. For the African American male growing up in the United States, everything he sees visually sends the blatant message: "You are the opposite of what's important in this land." For African American males, the only images the environment provided to them in America supports the illusions of sports or music being their only two paths to success.

Many Black males are growing up under this hostility to their soul and end up growing up with a "hood mentality." The sad part is the hood is in their hearts and even if they leave their neighborhoods, they take the hood with them. Some see being hood as a shield of armor so no one messes with them. Looking back, I see this shield for my own psyche was also harming me. It made me self isolate and prevented me from being able to discern (tell the different between) friend or foe.

America doesn't know how to embrace the African American boy. And sadly, he doesn't know how to embrace himself. This inability makes hostility towards those that look like himself an easy option. Isn't it normal to want to kill off the weak side of yourself? If you don't have a positive view of what you see in the mirror, it's not hard to imagine having an even harder time seeing value in those who resemble you.

Being in the enemy territory of the mind can lead to poor choices that are driven out of the human need to belong and feel secure. That's why even when athletes and entertainers reach their goals and attain wealth, internally they are still empty. Why? Because they never found out how to live in America as a man standing strong on his own merits. Instead, they bought into the illusion they would feel like a man once they had wealth.

To be a Black man and stand tall in America takes doing the hard, private work of defining one's self from the lens of faith, community, family, and intimacy. **Strength and balance for the Black man will not look like a White man's strength.** It will also feel different. And that's okay. In America, Black men will not always attain the wealth of what is perceived as financial success, but this cannot be the measuring stick of a man who has the world afraid of him. To me, when a Black man wakes up, he's already conquered half the world. To go to work and provide for his family is as powerful as conquering the universe. So to all the brothers living in America, I bow out of respect for the inner strength you have to gather each morning to simply open your eyes.

May the peace and blessing of Allah (God) continue to always be upon you.

AN AFRICAN PROVERB

"The child who is not embraced by the village will burn it down to feel warmth."

I f we continue as a culture and community to not find ways to embrace the boy-king energy in our Black boys, we will only reap their anger at us for not making them feel whole and connected. The concept of "gangs" is so limited in my eyes. That sense of belonging should come from those members' families! Why is it so hard to accept that even the most hardened killer started off as a person who simply wanted to be loved and accepted by their own people.

Black boys continue to burn our communities down daily each time they drop out of school, end a marriage, or leave their children never to return. This is very easy to do when you are never made to feel connected to the world in the first place. Where do Black boys turn to and can say, "I feel empty?" Or "I need a hug" or "I feel adrift in this large world"? My answer is sadly they often never have a place to turn. So is it so shocking this little boy grows up and hates everything that looks like him? Is it surprising he doesn't have the warmth or vision on how to see the beauty in the women with skin the color of his? Wouldn't you want as much distance as possible from the things that caused you the most pain when you where at your weakest?

I remember being called "an ugly thing" by Black girls growing up. As an older Man why would I be excited when the opportunity to marry a woman that reminded me of those girl came up? That would make me crazy. If Black boys are not taught better ways and options on how to express themselves and get loved back, then we have to prepare for larger fires because Black boys will continue to feel cold and burn our communities for the warmth we continue to deny them.

AIN'T NOBODY TELLING YOU

Ain't nobody telling you "no" but you! My brother Winston tells me that every morning when we have our morning check in and I begin to complain why something isn't going work and start making excuses on why I should give up. He always tells me it's my own thinking that's creating the issues, not the people involved. **He always reminds me that if I don't expect something to work out I will start designing and shaping my thoughts and then my actions to produce that outcome.** He encourages me to allow the opposite to be true. Allowing myself to assume the positive outcome is the only thing that will make things happen. When I do think in this way, it always surprises me how my thoughts go from black and white (yes or no) to thoughts of multiple outcomes and compromises.

Don't be the one telling yourself NO to your dreams. Don't be afraid to ask for exactly what you want out of life. As my mom would say, "A closed mouth don't get fed."

AM I AN ALPHA?

O n paper or for real? When I joined Alpha Phi Alpha in the spring of 2006, I was immediately shunned by a lot of brothers because of what I later learned was called a "paper process." The brotherhood didn't consider me a "real Alpha" because I didn't get hazed like they did. It was rough because I had and still have nothing but respect for them and admire their experiences.

What was difficult were the questions it generated in me and the insecurities it awoke! It caused me to do impersonal surveys when I went to Alpha functions. I would see who came in where and use that data to let me know who would accept my presence or who would turn their backs on me--and I do mean literally. I have literally had younger and older brothers refuse to speak to me if they knew I hadn't "pledged" like they had.

Looking back, it seems sad. Here are all these educated Black men, and we still where finding ways to exclude and alienate each other. It wasn't until I shared my feelings with Dr. Chambers (who is also an Alpha who pledged when pledging was not done underground). He said to me simply, "You're about to be a doctor, and you're worried about what young kids in undergrad think of you?"

That hurt, but it exposed a living wound that I have always tried to hide. The wound of never feeling accepted by the cool kids. Also, it questioned my toughness because I didn't go through the same rights of passage that they did. But where would it end? Wouldn't it then be someone else who would say my process was not as tough as theirs? **At some point, I had to accept that I determine all my definitions, and I write the meanings not others.** When I slip and let others write it for me, it will ALWAYS be skewed in a direction that gives them power over me!

I am an Alpha.

ARE BLACK BOYS ENCOURAGED TO HAVE A VOICE?

I don't think the world encourages Black boys to have a voice. I believe the world gives Black boys two options: 1. Be silent, or 2. Be an animal. **Black boys all have a voice, and it takes the village to give it a tone. A timbre.** Each Black boy is told by the world to be a whisperer. Be cool. Be silent and smooth. Sadly, none of these are true voices of expression. Most of them lead to silent little boys who feel unheard and unwanted. Who asks the caged Black boy why isn't he singing? Maybe that's why they all want to be rappers.

AS LONG AS I DON'T TRY, I CAN'T FAIL

All Black boys are at some point told they are smart (I Hope). The problem is that only a small few are SHOWN they are smart. I was always told I was smart. But it wasn't until I was an adult that I was shown by another Black man that I actually was smart. I was shown by one small but simple moment when I was asked by this man, "What do you think?" It was such a groundbreaking moment. Up until that point in my life, I don't recall anyone really asking my opinion as part of a decision that needed to made. That moment changed my life. It was the first time I felt what most people would term *respect*. I felt my opinion had value, and that, by extension, I had value.

Many Black boys go unseen and unasked. Mothers talk down to them. Women only see them as sex partners. The world sees them as predators.

But where is the voice of Black men? Do you really know what the Black men in your life think or feel moment to moment? This invisibility leads to a mental structure that allows failure to permeate. It makes the mind look for ways to fail instead of succeed. It makes the mind comfortable NOT trying to succeed. It makes pursuing new things feel odd and unnatural.

Sadly, for many Black men this becomes the only way they know to live. It's not out of not having a desire for a better life but instead it comes out of a belief that to try is to be exposed. To be vulnerable. And if the world tells you at every corner you have no value, ultimately for many Black men, it becomes easy to just accept that.

BREAKING YOU

If you feel God is trying to break you, I promise He is just doing what's needed to make you stronger. Make you accept He is trying to make you better. Make you build. Make you stronger. Make you know He's always with you. Make you know He's got you. Make you know **He will never leave you.** Make you know He will always love you. Make you know you're HIS child. Make you know you're worth it. Make you know He makes no mistakes. Make you know you're perfect at any moment He lets you breathe. Make you know He will always forgive you. Make you know He ain't goin' nowhere. Make you know He loves you unconditionally.

CONFLICT

Even as an adult, I find myself avoiding conflict. What is hilarious about this is I'm perceived as a person who confronts all issues. I like to think my truth is somewhere in the middle. I know I can be very direct at times. But those moments are often when I'm fed up. I think inherently I like peace. And I sometimes let myself get used to simply keeping the peace at all cost. What I have learned is some folks just don't know how to stop taking advantage of you, and **it's better to not keep a false peace if it hurts you inside (this is also called depression)**. I've learned that people truly see kindness as weakness.

Now to me that's a sad state of the world, but it doesn't mean nice people don't need to learn how to be a little selfish and feel comfortable taking care of themselves first. This leads to the best form of honesty in relationships. To truly be whole, it means being comfortable with others having a negative view of you and still being able to pursue the things that make you feel whole and happy. Too many times we delay or hide our dreams because those we love may be made to feel insecure because they may not have the talents you have. But you're God's child. He put you here to use what He gave you. He didn't put you here to ask those around you for permission before you start living your best life. DO YOU!

DO YOU BELIEVE
IN ME, MOMMY?

My wife took our 7-year old son to his second basketball practice. After the first practice, he started coming up with reasons why he didn't want to return. This was unusual for him. He is normally open to new events and people. So I decided to let it unfold instead of interrogating him. He said the coach said he needed to work on his shooting and that the other kids where "really good."

So my wife and I got into it because she said she had wanted to start working with him on his fundamentals years ago for basketball and I told her not to. (Sidebar: my wife grew up playing basketball her whole life and her father is a former Harlem Globetrotter.) I had asked my wife to hold off on basketball for two reasons. The first was because I wanted our son to just be a kid and play the game versus viewing it as a sport\job at 4 years old. The second reason was that I refuse to allow any of my children to ever believe sports is their only lane to success so I wanted him to get comfortable with school first.

So now he was at practice and was around kids who had been playing all their lives. Immediately he felt less than (at least that was my first thought). We had decided to try and find a sports league that was less competitive and that focused on skills development. On the day of the second practice, though, the coach called my wife. He asked if my son was coming. She said "No" and explained why. He encouraged my wife to bring him and comforted her by acknowledging her concerns but also reinforced there are larger gains by making him face his fears.

My wife then discussed it with me and we agreed he needed to not be allowed to give up. So on the way to practice, our son starts talking to my wife (this conversation was between a mother and her son. I was not present). He says to her his real reason for not wanting to return was because "those kids are cool and I'm not."

This was heart breaking. It took me back to how I felt growing up. All the feelings of weakness I had, feeling invisibility and isolation. However, what I think is at the root for my son at 7 and for me when I was at a lot of different ages is he doesn't feel Black (aka "cool") enough.

Oh, I didn't mention this basketball league is made up of all African-American boys. My son, like I did, goes to a private school. His private school is predominately White. Like me he is learning how to exist in both worlds (dual consciousness), and this was his first introduction. After sharing his truth to his mom about his fears, he asked her "Do you believe in me, mommy?" My wife being the best mom ever replied, "Hell, yeah, we are The Muhammad's, WE NEVER EVER give up!"

To me, I marvel at how much strength my son has to even be able to communicate that emotion and then ask for the support he needed from his mom. But how many Black boys need to know WE believe in them but never feel comfortable enough to take the risk and ask?

DON'T BE AFRAID
TO THIN THE HERD

One issue I struggle with is being successful. I especially feel this when I hear people discuss bills, health, and financial fears. Inside I'm not having those issues. I mean what do you do when what you just spend on a hotel room for one night an amount that would have paid your cousin's mortgage? What do you do when they can't pay that mortgage? Do you still go to the 5-star hotel for a night, just because? What I have learned is YES! I have to be able to reward myself for the decades of hard work I put in to have the options I have now.

Thinning the herd is a process most people who are successful must go through. I have learned that envy is inevitable. People will see what you have and ask themselves "Why him?" What they don't ask is, "How hard did he have to work to get there?" That's when you have to be able to not feel embarrassed or, in my case, guilty.

I have felt a deep guilt. Guilt to a point where I felt I had to say "Yes" when people ask for help. My close friend told me recently, **"People will use the money you give them for bills and their money for fun!"** That sentence gave me pause because it was true! Here I was pulling from my hard-earned savings to help someone and within hours I hear about them shopping at the mall when the day before they where crying to me about being evicted if they didn't get the money for rent. After enough of these events, I had to say enough is enough. I have the right to come first. And what happens to others is not my fault because I didn't create the crisis. As my friend Carl once said, **"We are all adults."**

DON'T BE STINGY
WHEN YOU'RE DOWN

When times get rough financially, it's the first reaction to hold on harder to what you have. I believe to show God that you riding with Him, you have to continue to give. Now I don't mean give all you have and hope things work out. What I'm suggesting is to give when you have a little extra. Someone always has it worst. I swear, I have giving thousands of dollars away when those closest to me needed it, and I never asked for it back. When I've been at my lowest, unfortunately the people I gave it to where not there for me. **What I can say is that God ALWAYS gave me what I needed in the most odd and always unpredictable ways and from people I least expected it to come from.**

I remember going to put gas in my truck, literally wondering how I was going to get food to feed my family dinner. I said, "Well, God, let me see how this will work out." And, I swear, I looked down on the ground and saw a 20-dollar bill!! Now, I'm not saying He's going to always give you plenty, but He will always give you enough.

DON'T CONFUSE
FEAR WITH DANGER

We are all telling ourselves a story. Fear is a choice. It is a product of our imagination that focuses on events that may never occur. Fear robs us of the moment by paralyzing us over events that may never happen in the future. YOU create the future. **If your core is fear-based, you are ensuring a future that is clouded by fear in every moment.** That's the devil. And the devil is always generated from within.

You can edit your story at any moment. **All the great people of our time found within themselves this truth and decided to stop asking others if they agreed.** Instead they decided to live and believe in themselves like they live and believed in God. Fear is the most powerful tool used by everyone afraid to take a risk. The greats throughout history simply believed that the true risk is not ever taking one.

If you find yourself running, please ask if your running from something that's not real. If you are, stop. STOP! Calm your mind! Calm your mind.

Trust that whatever your mind is telling you to fear will never be more powerful than your ability to face it and conquer it. You're God's child. He does not EVER set you up to fail. Ever. Even in moments when I thought I was losing, HE was preparing me to win on levels I could not ever imagine in my fears eyes. Fear limits options and prevents you from seeing the sun is coming up over the horizon.

DON'T LET ME
POP THE TRUNK

I ain't a killer, but don't push me. Growing up, I was sometimes bullied and I never fought back until I hit a limit and then something inside flipped and I blacked out. This way of being always made me feel weak. I felt weak compared to the stigma of Black men being willing to fight at the drop of a hat. I always thought I didn't have any strength. Then I spent decades reinforcing this fear by not speaking up for myself or hoping someone else would fight my battles.

As an adult, I now see it all differently. I now see I have always had self control. I have always tried to first think myself out of violent situations before reacting. Living within the African American community with my way of thinking made me an outsider. It made women look at me as weak because I didn't beat my chest and look for opportunities to fight.

My wife and I used to have heart-to-heart debates on the stupidity of fighting over your shoes being stepped on. Her position (at that time) was if we where out in public and if she felt disrespected, it was my **obligation** to confront the people involved and always defend her honor. My position was this was an unbalanced view and childish in the larger view of life and personal safety. To her, it was weak of me. It suggested to her that I should defend her. My point to her was that safety was first and **coming home alive was always the ultimate goal.**

As we have been together longer and now have children, her position has changed totally. She now sees that it takes a stronger man to swallow his pride and let disrespect pass so he can come home to his wife and family versus beating his chest and dying on a street corner over some trivial concept of what a man is.

FEAR

The majority of my life has been guided by fear. Multiple fears. Some rational, but the majority irrational. I believe to this day it keeps me from enjoying parts of my life, especially my successes. At the core of my fears is a feeling of not being strong enough. I accept as an adult this is normal, but I wonder if for an African American male child, it can be paralyzing. I wonder if the fears that where passed down to me where at one point in history necessary life skills for African American males but are no longer adaptive in our current society.

The fears I've had to overcome left me mentally locked. I always had an internal battle between my dreams and goals competing against what I was taught was not in my grasp. I take a different lens when I look at successful African American rappers. I believe African American males' attraction to them is the perception they are independent thinkers. Masters of their lives and fate. I believe rappers are the most accessible example for young African American males of what they themselves can accomplish if they just believe.

I don't believe, for example, that academia is attractive to young African American males because those successful in it are not as visible as rappers. Not only visible on TV but also in their immediate neighborhoods.

Rappers promote an elevated sense of confidence, unlimited money, and access to the social riches of life. I mean who wouldn't want that? They also **LOOK** fearless! For these reasons, I get it. What is missing is substance and depth. For me, my fears were not going to be overcome by watching rap videos (but I admit for several years they did or I thought they would!). My goals needed different types of models and examples.

As a human, I accept that I will always have fears. What I've learned as I've gotten older is that fear is a convenient excuse to do nothing with your life. A common saying I heard growing up was "The White man won't let us..." This statement never felt true to me. Now, please understand, I know racism and prejudice exist. I've been faced with it many times. What is not true about that statement is how often it is applied to in many African Americans lives as a real justifications to give up.

For example, the White man does not stop you from getting an education or starting your own businesses. **YOU STOP YOU!** I can honestly and, with certainty, say that it is was often people that did not look like me, be it race or gender, that did what they could to help me get where I am in life.

Case in point. My first year of graduate school I rewarded myself with starting my dread locks. It was a reward because I had told myself I would never be able to find a job in San Diego if I had dread locks due to the social stigma **I believed** came with them (see there goes that fear again). Coincidentally as soon as I started them, I gave into the social pressure of my classmates who where seeking research assistant jobs and decided to try and get me one! Well, given my limited connections and almost nonexistent resume, I didn't have any hookups to get me a spot so I did what any hustler would do. I looked on Craigslist! (Smile). (This was 2001 so Craigslist was everything at that time. This was before all of the millions of job listing sites existed like they do today). And guess what? I got an interview.

But here is where it gets interesting. The interview was at a hospital in the San Francisco Bay area. I think: I'll go to interview, get denied but at least be able to say to my classmates I tried. I go to the interview and make it to the second round. Remember now, I just started my dread locks. (For those of you who don't know that when you first start your locks and they are in small separations, they make your scalp look like a checkerboard!) So here I am, crazy hair and all, at a job interview.

42

Well guess where the second interview was? **STANFORD University!!** Yes!! What the people at Stanford had done was list the job on Craigslist instead of the university's job board to attract somebody like me! A minority who looked like the people in the study they wanted to recruit! **(God is good, and God is a comedian!).** So as soon as I faced my fear of expression via my hair, God rewarded me with a job that wanted me literally because I looked like ME!

The woman in charge was a White woman. And let me tell you, she mentored me for the next 7 years until I graduated, and she kept me out of harm's way many times and fought for me when I couldn't for myself. So the concept of the White man keeping me down is a mindset I challenge daily. **I believe often it is the person you see in the mirror that is keeping you down (BUT YOU ALSO HAVE ALL THE POWER YOU NEED TO LIFT YOU UP!!).** I believe, unlike any other time in the world, opportunity is endless for all minorities. We just have to be prepared when it arrives. What I mean is I didn't just get the job at Stanford because of my skin color, I was also pursuing my Ph.D. in Psychology and understood the research they where conducting. That's preparation meeting opportunity.

FIND WHAT FEEDS YOU

Don't go to McDonald's expecting to get fresh vegetables. What I mean is in life we often have people in our families, like our mothers and fathers, who we will run to in emotional crisis and need and want their comfort and calm. Sometimes they just won't have it to give. It doesn't mean they don't love you, but the emotional meal you need may have to come from someone else. And that's okay. The one thing you can't do is starve. Find what feeds you and get fed.

FIRED

One thing I've had to learn to live with is getting fired. I been fired so many times it's like a ritual. Sometimes I deserved it. I'd say most times I deserved it. A few times people wanted to show me who had the power. Over the years what hurt the most is when it was another African American firing me out of pure pettiness. One time I got fired because I wouldn't go have drinks with my male boss. It was later discovered he was a sexual predator who used his position of authority to get sex.

Getting fired can either break you or motivate you. Getting fired is all about how you interpret it. Do you tell yourself it was the only job in the world? Do you say they are losers? It's a million labels you can choose. What's critical is that you don't mistakenly own someone else's issues. What I mean is oftentimes when working for other people, they can see your potential.

Unfortunately, a lot of people's insecurities get activated by this and it leads them to viewing you as competition, which in their minds becomes a threat to their authority. So they begin to make up stories in their minds about you, such as "They think they're all that." or "They think they're better than me." These cognitions (silent thoughts) are ultimately played out in their actions. The final action is them firing you.

I had to learn to see these moments as a way to connect with my faith and understand something better was already coming. It's, of course, hard to do that when you have bills to pay, but honestly what choice did I have? Either I sat and moped and fed into that negative energy or I could focus that energy in a positive direction and reassert the truth: **Only God can fire me!**

GO FIND THE BULLY

My philosophy on life is if you know the bully is coming for you, go looking for them! I truly believe that to get over a fear, you have to stop running from it and confront it.

I've found that the biggest bully is inside me. **I often bully myself into fear.** I'm often the one who's stalking down my own thoughts and crushing them or making them feel impossible. If you know a bully is waiting for you after school, sometimes you gotta leave class early, go find you a brick, and go looking for him!! Most bullies (fears) lose all their heart when they see you are not afraid.

The first few times I stood up to my fears, I've been full of anxiety, heart racing, stomach churning. But dang!

When I wasn't facing the fear, I felt even worse!! So I often back my own self into a corner and tell myself **I'm suffering at my own hands** and that has to stop. So that's when I start looking for the bully!

GOD NEVER YELLS.
HE WHISPERS

So, you have to learn to be quiet inside to hear Him. If you hear a voice that's yelling, it's probably the devil masquerading as fear.

The journey of life is about family and happiness. The illusion of growing up in America challenges this belief daily. Being an African American male at a young age is even harder because you feel a constant pressure of being behind even before you start.

Money is only a tool. It took me awhile to learn something. One day I realized I really don't care about money. What I realized I care about is having options. I want options to sleep in. Travel. Shop. Eat healthy. To have these options I have to have money. But thank God, I've been broke and broken enough times to know now that money can't fix all sad days. It can only give you a softer couch to cry on.

A lot of my best moments came when I had nothing. That's always when I found out who loved me most. Just know God has never made money in the bank a test of how much favor He will bless you with. God is more saddened by you not doing all you can with the gifts He's given you than how well you look in church on Sunday.

The fastest way to disappoint God is to worry. Worrying means you're doubting God and placing limits on how much He can change your life or ease your pains. The fastest way to celebrate the breathes He gives you is to breath life into your dreams.

GROW

L ittle brother, grow.

Please feed your mind with things that create growth like comic books and Black Panther movies. (Yes, you read that right.) Please never surrender your imagination. Play. Then play some more. Grow in the directions that feel right.

If you love books, then love them! Read a million of them. Read widely. Read vast.

If music is your joy, then explore all the world offers.

I just beg of you to grow. **Never accept or listen to anything that feels like a limit.** When someone tells you that you can't do something, it just means they couldn't so they doubt you can either. That means they chose to stop growing. Plant seeds in your mind and water them with experiences. But whatever you do, please grow!

HOW DO I KNOW
I'M BECOMING A MAN?

To be honest, I still don't know! I'm currently 42 years old. I have a wonderful wife and four boys. And yet, I still feel like a young boy learning about life. When I was a child, I assumed by the age I am now it would be all smooth sailing and the path would be clear.

Man, what I'm learning is even the best of us are still facing struggles! When I was young, I thought to become a man, you start to feel a least a little more comfortable taking risks and being able to learn from the results and still find ways to go forward. Being a man to me now is more about being a leader of my family. But sometimes being that leader also means being able to follow and submit to good advice. It also means being able to set goals and pursue them even when those close to you just don't get it. For example, part of being a man to me is setting goals that I know, in the long run, will benefit my family. There have been times when I didn't have the full support of my wife, but I knew what I was doing was right for us in the long run and I just had to take that walk alone.

Now, I know the men I looked up to when I was younger took many walks alone in their minds while pursuing goals. What I especially see now as manly is they didn't let it make them resent their families for not knowing how to offer support when they needed it the most. Instead, they dug deep inside and found that voice they knew to trust and kept walking.

One time my wife told me my mother shared with her that she was happy that when I was setting goals for my life, I ignored her advice about getting "a steady job" instead of working for myself because if I had listened to her I wouldn't be providing the quality of life I am now and will for my family.

As a man I have learned a lot of the times when someone close to me is suggesting I delay a dream, they are sometimes doing it because when they tried to pursue a dream, it didn't work out for them. Sometimes they just don't want to see you getting disappointed.

But for someone crazy like me, the process is always where my largest growths have come from. I will learn nothing if I always succeed immediately. I literally start off a lot of plans by simply stating, "I want to do... and I have no idea what I'm doing, but I'm about to find out." From there I say a prayer and start my grind. I've done this repeatedly over the years.

I also try to avoid people who need to plan into paralysis. I avoid people who need to have a million meetings before doing anything. The movers and shakers of the world don't have time to meet all week. Why? Because they are out in the world taking risks and seeing what happens versus sitting around planning to make it happen.

HOW I EXPERIENCE GOD

I am amazed at how I am often judged because of my faith. My wife calls me a heathen when I tell her to tell Jesus I said, "What's up?" for me when she goes to church. Though I don't always feel heavily religious, I feel VERY spiritual.

I remember trying to explain how I experience God to a very close friend, and it turned into a debate. There position was that each experience I shared was one they felt compelled to connect to a Bible verse. And they also constantly invited me to their church to the point I felt pressured.

These experiences are not new to me, but they do make me sad. They make me sad because even those that I know who love me often cannot find a way to embrace our differences. Often, I feel I can make more room for them than they can for me. I love that all people can experience God their own personal way. What I dislike is the need to judge me if I don't follow the path that calls to them.

I explained to my friend that to me God is active and alive in every breath I take. I feel God in simple moments when I can't find something and a clarity comes over me that wasn't there before that allows me to find what was just invisible. God to me is when I have no gas in my truck and no idea how I am going to feed my family and I literally look on the ground and see $20 that wasn't there before I started talking to God. God is also with me during my times of pain. He's the calm I need when I can't find it.

For me, scriptures don't always speak to my soul like a YouTube sermon from TD Jake's. Or a "Never could have made it" by Warren Sapp. In those moments, I feel my closest to God. I feel He wants us to be our own God. He wants us to have faith in ourselves like we have faith in Him.

In this journey, we have been made to believe it is arrogance and conceit to have faith in yourself beyond what others permit you to believe. **I believe it's an act against God if we don't believe we can do anything.** Man places limits, not God. To me, faith is the most powerful tool we are armed with.

To make anyone feel that a personal choice of faith is less than someone else's is simply a sign the other person has serious insecurities. A true believer knows God has many shapes, sizes, languages, and colors. **To limit His power is to limit what you believe He can do for you.**

I SELF LORD AND MASTER.

HOW TO SURVIVE
AS A UNICORN

I'm a unicorn. I'm what the world says can never exist.

I'm an African American male, doctor, father, husband, brother, and son, with no criminal record. I teach at an historically Black college. I have my own private practice. I'm heterosexual.

What's even deeper is I know a ton of other Black men just like me!! Sadly, I'm considered, even inside my own culture, a unicorn, rare, special, not likely to happen again. And that's just not true!

I've survived in this life due to those around me seeing the value in investing in me. Loving me. Supporting me. I also survived because I sought out and found other Black men who were doing what I wanted to do as an adult, THRIVE. **I didn't accept not having my father around as a reason to not push myself.** I didn't limp through life and make myself a victim. I decided that, yes, having a father to assist and guide me would be ideal, but I also looked around the world and saw successful men from ALL cultures who have made it in life without being blessed to have a supportive father along their path.

Being a unicorn means knowing God has given you a purpose even when you don't know what it is. You survive by taking the paths that are driven from what's inside of you.

There are herds of us unicorns out there. We aren't as rare they people think.

HYPERSEXUALITY

I was having a deep conversation with a DJ friend of mine. We were sharing or experiences growing up male and without a father inside the African American culture. He made a great point that reframed for me years of pain.

I recalled the decades of torment I received from other males whenever I was hurt by being dumped or by something a woman said about my looks. I was told by other males to forget about her or just plain: "Dump that Bitch and go find you another one." But for me that never calmed the painful feelings I was having. It actually only made them worse because I felt I was damaged and because I could not control or dismiss my emotions like the majority of the other males around me did (or pretended to be able to). They all seemed so unaffected by women or the ending of the relationships with them.

My friend reframed this life view I had held for many years in one simple statement. He said, "Man, that's all a mask to hide their own emotions that by using hyper-masculinity as an overcompensation for their own underdeveloped emotions." Bam! Wow! It was all so clear now.

It rewrote that whole script. It wasn't that they didn't have the same emotions. It was simply that they where stuffing them away. Now don't get me wrong. I was still more sensitive than the average guy, but this one friend's comment made me feel closer to normal years later in my adulthood.

What I see now is that many males like me are made to feel isolated from the pack. What I also see is that from this isolation many of the world's thinkers have been created (e.g. Malcom X, Martin Luther King Jr., Christopher L. Edwards).

I DON'T KNOW
HOW TO SAY THIS

Being in a relationship with a woman was always hard for me. I was always able to attract women, but once I got them I never felt like I had anything inside to keep them. For a long time I was always afraid and intimidated when it came to dating women who had college degrees. I look back and believe this came from a fear of being discovered for what I felt inside, which was empty.

Women always called me "sensitive." (My wife calls me that all the time and now I just laugh inside because I know it's where my strength comes from). Growing up and being called sensitive was like being called weak. I still don't know why anyone would want to make me feel weak and I wonder if they were jealous of something I had inside that they knew they would never have. Being called sensitive by a woman you are in love with always generated a tornado of emotions and often lead me to hide and withdraw.

I now look at myself and see my being caring and nurturing as some of my greatest traits. I now believe that when someone calls me sensitive, it's often (not always) coming from a place inside them that is underdeveloped and not able to see the spiritual value of caring about how others feel.

My son's are sensitive, and I love it! And anyone will tell you if you want to see me volcanic, just try to make my kids feel bad about crying or expressing their feelings. I refuse to allow my children (four boys) to be made to feel less than like I was just because they are smart and can express in words when they have been hurt or disappointed. I tell my boys everyday: **"Don't let anyone get in your head, and if you're not sure about what you're thinking or feeling, just come ask Daddy."**

This is important to me as part of their own foundation. **I want them (and you the reader) to be able to trust their own thoughts and dreams and be able to turn down the noise that will inevitably come from those around them.** In intimate relationships I want my son's to be able to never lose their internal compass while also being deeply connected to another person.

In my early relationships I was always anxious and worried about being left. What I've learned and what I will always teach my boys is: **YOU are the prize!**

I HATED WHEN
MY FATHER DRANK

I remember before my father passed, he went to rehabilitation (rehab). I prayed it would fix the marriage problems my parents were having and he would be happy. Looking back I know see I'm a lot like my father was: sensitive. He was caring and in love with his kids. But to this day, I still don't know all the demons that lead him to drink his pains away.

I remember when my parents would have house parties and he would call me to him and tell me to do the latest dance I knew. It was always embarrassing. But not in a way a child feels when performing for adults. It was an embarrassment that came from feeling awkward that everyone seemed to know this was only entertainment for my dad's drunken state.

My dad was an alcoholic. He was also a policeman, and somehow he found away to go to cosmetology school and became a cosmetologist so he could do my sisters hair. I share all that to say he was not just one thing. Most of all, he was a human who had struggles.

For me, life has always been heavy because I always feared I had some flaw deep inside that would one day become activated and cause me to loose control and kill myself like my father did. I have lived my life always in fear of loosing control. So to brace for this inevitable event I felt would happen, I learned to not overreact, act like nothing bothered me, and to look stoic at all cost or injury. What this had done to me as an adult is make it hard to show love and affection or to share with others when I'm in pain.

I now know these are important things all Black men have issues with as we become men. I believe as Black men a lot of our anger and "coolness" is how me mask our depression and anger about real or perceived invisibility in the world and often in our own homes. For Black men, we have to master speaking while also being invisible (so as not to make anyone scared or uncomfortable). This type of living causes a functional insanity, where you're alive but not allowed to live.

My challenge now is to make sure my boys know and feel they have a voice worth being heard. I want to make sure they have a confidence inside they will trust and use as a compass on how to find their own paths. I don't want them to give into the invisible pressures the world applies on them by subtle messages, such as Black men should play sports, chase women, do drugs, and not pursue higher education. **I tell my boys that it's okay to want to play on the team, but I'm raising them to know they can also own the team.**

I LOVE THINKING NEGATIVE

I started reading a lot of material on the power of positive thinking. I asked myself why I start off my day by consistently focusing on what I wanted to worry about. The word "wanted" is significant because I realized I was making a choice. I could think positively or negatively. I had surrendered my thinking to negativity out or pure habit and cognitive laziness.

I now realize by thinking negatively I will always have built-in excuses to not do the work. To give up. To not really try. The bottom line is your life and levels of success are based on what you press PLAY on in your mind. If the mental tapes you have are heavy with negative thoughts, then, guess what, your outcomes will be covered with negative outcomes.

As I practice a new way of thinking, I feel odd, like I'm doing something foreign to my natural system. And in reality I am. For so much of our life we have controls that we never utilized. Positive thinking is a crucial tool that has to be practiced daily. I promise it works!!

I OUTGREW YOU

The hardest thing I have battled is outgrowing people I've looked up to. I looked up to mentors like they were dads and always expected them to have more to teach me. **My mom always said "sometimes people are only meant to be in your life for a reason or a season"** and, lawd have mercy, I hated when she said that! It was because I wanted everyone to stay forever.

Looking back I see I kept some people around WAY too long. I see that I outgrew many of my mentors. But what caused this was often that they themselves stopped growing. They stopped pushing themselves. For me, this often contradicted the things they taught me about life and pursuing my goals.

One thing I'm not is a lair. And no matter how well worded you dress it a lie is a lie. So if you're mentoring me and tell me to always work hard and never give up. When you give up, I feel lied to. At the core of that is I think I have a hard time accepting even those I look up to are also human.

So I'm saying to you, the reader, that outgrowing anyone you look up to is part of your growth process. It doesn't mean you have to forget what they taught you. What it means is you have to give yourself continuous freedom to move on!

One of my mentors used to tell me I was inpatient. And he was and is correct. What I took issue with is that he never asked me why. For me, I will always be impatient because I refuse to live a life based on the assumption that what is here today as an opportunity will be here tomorrow.

That same mentor went through a tragic downfall in his life and later said to me, "I really fell off my game, and if I could, I would do a lot of things differently." One of the things I'm sure he would do differently is not assume his opportunities would always be in reach. It hurts me still because I warned him to look at the blessing in front of him and take advantage of it. But his response was, "I can always create more." That is great, but it's just not always possible because the universe is always in motion and it does not wait for anyone.

I see it was in those moments I was outgrowing him and didn't even know it. The growth and distance was coming from me not being able to stand still with him while everything in my journey was telling me to move, hustle, grind and explore. So always be fair to yourself and your inner voice and don't let feelings of guilt or loyalty make you ignore your journey. You can never outgrow yourself, only other people.

I'M NOT GOING TO
DISCRIMINATE AGAINST ME

Many times growing up, there was always an undercurrent of thought (unconscious) in my mind that only White people could get or have certain jobs in San Diego where I lived (or the world for that matter). I believed these jobs where reserved just for them. Later on I realized I had incorporated this into my own psyche whenever I thought about a career or even a summer job. For example, growing up I only remember seeing White or Latino people working in Footlocker, the shoe store. So when I moved to the South (North Carolina) as an adult, I was blown away when I saw African Americans working in those stores, in every store.

Unconsciously, I had developed a low level tier system based on where I thought my dreams could reach. Just think about it. I didn't even think I could even dream about working at the Gap! Think about the level and depth of discrimination I had applied to myself. Think about ALL the places I told myself I would never be hired at so I didn't even bother applying.

I became the person discriminating against myself! I became the "They won't let us" in my own mind. I know many of us still live and believe in this self defeating way. I even see it with my wife, my sister, and even my mother (all of them I know can do anything they want if they just decide).

Sometimes, I believe the biggest things God blessed me with is a high IQ and a high capacity to be too dumb to listen. What I mean is often times I just decide to ignore the crowd and test the water. And many of my life's victories have come from this way of living. I also believe it shows God is in not only my words but also my actions. This makes me truly have faith in Him even when I scared and uncertain.

I now just go for things and let the chips fall where they may. I'm now applying for anything I want. Scholarships, grants, loans etc. **If you're scared to do something, I say do it because your scared!** Growth often comes from facing our biggest fears.

I don't allow my mind to live in a world where every dream a White man has comes true for him just because they are White. I realize Whites also suffer and experience poverty and, yes, discrimination, but in a different way. I want to again be clear that I'm in no way saying White privilege does not exist. What I am saying is the privilege of being **God's Child** is always going to be more powerful and always more unconditional than any imagined limit or fear your mind creates.

I'M BEHIND IN MY BILLS
AND MY DREAMS

Keep running towards your dreams and away from fear. Are you behind on your bills and your dreams? It's sad and also funny how these both always go hand in hand. Rich people are rich because they believe they should be. Poor people stay poor because they don't believe another way is possible for them.

Dream big and whatever you accomplish will always put you closer to your dreams than had you done nothing. **Excellence is a habit and so is failure.** Are you choosing to fail?

Pride causes paralysis. Pride keeps you from asking for help to get to the next step of your dreams. The illusion poor people suffer under is they should do it alone. **The reality of rich people is they will call a million people until they get the answer they need.**

The struggle is what will make you. Focused struggle. It's not getting knocked down that makes you. It's the process of getting up that builds new parts inside your soul that will help you succeed.

Please know that God answers all prayers. What most people are not prepared for is sometimes He says, "No." God's plans are often painful and delayed. I remember prayers that seemed unanswered showed themselves 10 years later and better than I had expected. Trust in Him and always trust your process. No plan He has for you is to hurt you or keep you down. Keep knowing He wants the best for you. He didn't bring you this far to drop you off here!! You keep standing! No matter what, don't give up!

I'M HITTING A WALL I DON'T KNOW HOW TO CLIMB

When you feel like you are hitting an emotional wall or limit you can't climb over, please just stop. The compulsion will be to rush to find a solution or even give up. Patience is the best tool in these moments (and God will provide plenty of these moments). **Patience is the same as active faith when you don't know what else to do.**

Calm yourself. CALM YOURSELF. Gather your ability to focus and then start to look for solutions. If none come immediately, then ask God for it. That's why He's there! Sometimes we treat God like a friend you can only ask a favor from once and awhile. That's not the relationship God offers us. He gives us unlimited favors in return for our unlimited belief He will answer all of them. Sometimes we just have to quiet ourselves to hear His answer even if it's "No."

There is never a real wall outside of the one you created in your mind's fear. Let go of the fear and the wall goes away immediately.

I'M SURE THE RIGHT TOOL WILL START GLOWING WHEN I NEED IT

Preparation and prayer matter. Do the hard work. Do what scares you. Do what others think is impossible to do or duplicate. Learn to be your own counsel. Accept that great leaders often start their journey alone. Know that doubt is normal and giving up is easy.

This life is not a dress rehearsal. There are no do overs.

Ask yourself what you want (don't ask why); then go get it! Don't over plan. Don't over think. Just do it! So many people mask their fears by getting bogged down in planning and delays.

I have always believed if I put out the effort and energy behind a dream, the dream will become reality. I have also learned it's important to asked for help and guidance. When I am told "No," I just find another person to ask until I get a "Yes." Like the old saying goes: "A closed mouth doesn't get fed." **You don't ask you don't get!**

I'M THE WEIRDO

I'm the weirdo because I open doors for women. Because I want to read a book. But the thugs were the standard growing up.

Ultimately, I grew up feeling invisible and with continuous low self-esteem. I believe I'm what should be the standard for all Black men and not the **Outcast**.

But sadly, the worst example of what Black men could be is often promoted. That ideal is "Catch the ball, son." That's easy! Teaching a Black boy how to be a man and provide for their family is hard!

IN THE LONELY ROOM

College started off bumpy to put it gently. I bounced from one community college to another and changed my major daily. I believe a large part of it was due to not having a sense of direction.

College was a lonely journey in the beginning. I believe in large part it was due to not having anyone that looked like me in my classrooms or as instructors. To me, all my classmates seemed so on the ball. I felt isolated. Incompetent. An imposter. (I later discovered the imposter syndrome is a common and debilitating experience of minorities pursuing higher education.)

The lonely room can become the peaceful palace. This process is about facing your fear of flying—or in my case, my fear of succeeding.

Growing up without a father, I think left me constantly seeking the approval of other males. In the normal rites of passage, I believe a son grows under his father's eyes until he eventually reaches a point where the father gives his blessing and tells the son he can fly on his own. As a grown man, I wanted that the rite of passage. But now, I see I have to give myself that permission to fly.

Many Black boys have to learn to give themselves and others that permission to fly. Sometimes it may even come from someone younger than you who has already been blessed with that permission.

FLY. You can do it! Each day gives you an opportunity to soar and find new heights. The lonely room is only a temporary place once you learn that the permission you seek has to come from inside.

JUST BECAUSE YOU'RE BY YOURSELF DOESN'T MEAN YOU'RE ALONE

Going through my younger life I always felt alone. When I was by myself, I always felt vulnerable. I was so vulnerable and full of fear I used to be afraid to go to malls. I was always afraid of getting beaten up. Not that this ever happened. It was just a fear I made up. I would think of the thing I feared most and prepare my day like it was going to happen. It was sort of like living in a bomb shelter of my mind. I missed so many opportunities to hangout. To have fun. To be free. All out of fear.

I thought I was alone. I thought those that smiled at me were eventually going to make fun of me. Yet, I always took others' opinions of me over my own opinion of myself. Always. What's funny is this was always counter to the feedback I was getting from the world. I was always being called "cute" or "smart." But my rationale was off. If ten (TEN!) fine-butt girls called me "cute," it still didn't have the power of one (ONE!) ugly girl calling me a "skinny nerd."

As a man, I now have to ask myself what existed in my psyche then that made my mind chase the negative. This type of thinking can only inevitably make you feel alone and depressed. Even in a crowded room. I think the fear then was being exposed as having feelings. Even to this day my wife calls me "sensitive." And it used to sting. It was like having a Scarlet Letter on my manhood. Sensitive meant "less than" to me.

Not tough. Almost feminine.

Now I see it as my greatest power. What I now understand is that sensitive souls are not pack beings, subject to the whims of the herd. Sensitive souls by design are like Jesus. They come with a message that won't be understood by the masses in the moment. Sensitive Kings will always walk alone.

I'm here to say that to any young brothers walking alone: You have the peace of knowing you're walking by yourself but you're never alone. You got me!

LONELY AT THE BOTTOM

Often, it's been said it's lonely at the top. I found it was lonely at the middle and at the bottom. At any level what I have had to change was my definition of loneliness. Loneliness used to feel like isolation. It was a self-induced time out.

As I have grown, I view my time alone (both mentally and physically) as priceless. The times I thought everyone I knew in the world was out having a great time without me I now reflect back and see those were some of the best times of my life (so far). During those times alone (no girlfriends, no close homies to spend time with), I was growing. I was developing my own views of the world without the interference (noise) of others. I see now that those who had a bunch of friends also had a bunch of noise in their lives. Being by myself allowed me to start a thought and finish it on my own time and along my own path. The conclusions I developed where unique (sometimes flawed), but they were mine! Not the village's. And they weren't open to scrutiny. That has extreme value even to this day.

I was my own best friend before it became popular to be "into yourself. I was developing a foundation that still serves me today.

MEN ARE TAUGHT TO FEEL
FRAGILE IF THEY CRY

I think we (Black men) are fragile because we don't cry. I think women gather a lot of strength from being able to purge themselves through the release that comes from shedding tears. A study was done on the chemical makeup of happy versus sad tears, and they found tears have two different chemical makeups. The body even knows the difference. This suggests to me the body uses tears to allow certain things to be expelled from the body, including pain.

So, if men never cry, imagine all the hurt and pain that remain stored and circulating in the life of their body. Think about how when kids cry, they so quickly process what happen, repair it in their minds and hearts, and move on. Think about how we as men would be more open to the joys of life if we allowed ourselves this very human experience. I wonder if us not crying has any connection to why women outlive us. Just a thought...

MERCEDES

I remember the first time I met Dr. Chambers. I was referred to him because I was experiencing depression but didn't know it. Fortunately, someone noticed my symptoms and pointed me to him.

When I arrived at his office, I wasn't sure I had the correct place. First, the "office" was actually in a house in a residential area that had been converted into an office space. And there was a huge Mercedes-Benz parked in the driveway. I assumed I was going to see a White doctor.

When I entered the building, there was no one to great me so I just came inside and sat down. About five minutes after coming in, a nicely Black man came down the stairs and changed one of the bags in the small trash can in the waiting area. I thought he was the janitor until he introduced himself as Dr. Chambers. Immediately, I thought: Oh man, here we go; he's a low budget doctor. But I was willing to see where it went and followed him upstairs to his office.

By the time the session was over, I was immediately feeling better and comfortable! So much so that I asked him whose car was outside and why he had decided to rent a house instead of renting a traditional office space.

His reaction was priceless!! He calmly said, **"That car outside is mine, and I own this building."**

I was speechless. I never even considered a Black man could legally operate on the financial level he was on (AND STILL IS TO THIS DAY!). I was always told that educated people are basically poor and work to pay off student loans for the rest of their lives. He was and is still one of the richest people I know both financially and emotionally. I still wasn't able to accept his words initially so I pressed further. I said, "Hey, I saw a White man in one of the other offices downstairs. Is he your boss?"

Dr. Chambers laughed and replied, "No, he's my business partner."

What?! This man had a White man as his business partner! And I later had the opportunity to get to know his business partner (Dr. Lee), and he is also amazing. He and I had a once had a 3 hour about what it's like to be White that changed my life.

I wasn't convinced yet so I asked Dr. Chambers for some clarification. "So, you mean you don't have a boss? You don't have to be somewhere at a certain time for someone else?"

He replied, **"No, I don't have a boss. I'm my own boss. I set my own schedule, and I decide when and how hard I want to work each day."**

Man, I was hooked! I knew then this was the lane I wanted to be in. It took 13 years and many, many tears, but like Dr. Chambers **I am now my own boss.** I set my own schedule and decide how much and how hard I want to work. **All it took was just seeing that it was possible for a Black man and that it was possible for me.**

Along my entire professional relationship with him, Dr. Chambers has always said two things: 1. **"Rules are for poor people"** and 2. **"The best way to repay me is to be better than me. Make so much money you make me look poor."** That's love. That's true mentorship.

MY BEST FRIEND

For some retarded reason my friend Kisha supported me from the moment I met her when I was in the 9th grade on a community access television show where we were the featured dancers. After High School she started attending community college, and I just sort of followed her lead but not with as positive results as she had (at first).

Kisha taught me how to use going to college as a hustle. First it was how to get a nice financial aid check while getting a college degree. What's so interesting looking back is we really had no guidance other than good intentions. God truly loves babies and fools. Kisha taught me how to get financial aid, how to get my classes paid for by the state of California via grants, and how to use school programs to get priority registration. Man! Straight up hustle!

Kisha always had money in her pocket!! I always didn't! We laugh now at how we used to have to "dig in the ashtray." You ain't lived until you had to dig in the ashtray of your car and take all the coins to the gas attendant and ask for **"Three dollars on pump 5."** Lawd have mercy, those where the best days! They were the best because they really made us learn the value of a dollar. We learned to hustle and save. Now mind you, I didn't have a lot saved, but I always kept some emergency coins in the ashtray for that emergency date I didn't plan for (emergency date is another way of saying booty call).

My best friend graduated with her second master's degree on July 8, 2017, in marriage and family therapy. This was such a major event in her life! She faced so many fears to get it. It was literally a 20-year process. It took 18 years to get emotionally ready to do it, and two years to complete the program. But imagine how strong she had to be to take the first step! Well, this is the person I leaned on during all my dramas. And thanks to her letting me peek in on her 20-plus-year marriage, I am now a much stronger husband. I learned from watching her marriage that it's not always a honeymoon but we can overcome anything. This was a major advantage for a romantic like me.

To be balanced, you have to have people who will tell you when YOU smelling yourself. Well, I developed that support early on and ended up marrying a woman that tells me I stink daily! (Smile).

MY DAILY AFFIRMATION

The following is my daily affirmation. My brother suggested I create it during a time I needed to know **from myself** I had positive value at a time I was questioning if I should stay around. I encourage anyone who reads mine below to create their own. At some point in all our lives we need to speak to ourselves about the best parts of ourselves. This is my affirmation to myself.

I am the last dragon. I am the warrior I been hoping would protect me my whole life. I have always been more than good enough. I am perfect. I am God's child, always have and been always will be. I am strong. I am still standing. I am not afraid. Any fear I have is a fear I created. My thoughts are perfect. It's doubt that corrupts them.

You always thought you where alone, but you where actually free. You can pray anything away. Faith is contagious. Let it infect you. And try to infect others with yours.

Life has challenges, but none you cannot face. None. I don't need the world to validate me. I validate me. It doesn't mean others' opinions are not wanted. I just can't let theirs be the loudest voices in my life. Life has been hard. But it has been fun.

Your kids need you. Your wife needs you. Your kids love you. You need to love you unconditionally and never fucking ever let the challenges created by man make you doubt your faith in the power of God! Have faith in yourself. STOP asking to borrow faith from others. Your decisions have always led you down the correct path even when the path looked dark.

You can talk heaven into existence by simply saying it. So say it! Say it now! Choose to believe instead of choosing to doubt. Think the positive outcome will always happen!

When you believe the best will happen the best will happen. God didn't bring you this far to drop you off here! I am the master of my fate and truly the captain of my soul. It is not our enemies that defeat us, it is our fear. Make THEM afraid of you! The biggest mistake I ever made was doubting myself.

MY EGO

I never thought I had a large ego. But I do. **My ego kicks in when someone tells me I can't do something.** Then something inside of me says "Fuck them," and my mind immediately starts to plan.

It wasn't until my mom told me recently when I was telling her I want to buy a home but didn't think I'd ever be able to (my credit has always not been good enough). My mom replied, "The only reason you haven't bought a house yet is because you haven't decided to. I have never seen you not get what you want when you put your mind to it."

I immediately was angry. I was angry because she wasn't being my mom: she was being my rock. My mother and I have always been that for each other even when I was a child. We always have our **cut-the-bullshit conversations** when it was needed. And she took the shot often, and it hurt because it always hit the mark. It hurt because it was true, and she hit my ego. But, man, what's the point of an ego if it's not used to motivate you passed your own shit!

So, I took the time to go over my life challenges, and I see my ego is not one that is easily visible. When I used to think of ego, I thought of sports players or entertainers. These were people who wanted to be seen, people who thrive for attention and beat their chests and roar to the crowd. I have learned there are silent warriors like me and President Obama (yes he has a LARGE ego) that keep their ego hidden but always available.

My ego has an "I'll make you choke on your fuckin' words" style. So many times, I did shit just 'cause someone thought the skinny kid with glasses couldn't. And sometimes that meant fucking their girlfriend (smile).

As an adult (insert laugh), I'm more mature now. I focus my goals now on things I feel or felt where impossible and make them goals. I see know the limits of my ego are simply set by my own fears and limited vision. **The beauty of the ego is its fearless.** It has no conscience, and the only person it cares about is you! For a caring person like me, it's sometimes hard to make goals that don't serve other people first. The ego says "Do you" and "Be happy." I've learned this is okay. Being a child of God, I have worked on not being responsible for the happiness of others and worked to magnify the gift of life God has blessed me with by being happy with life without guilt and let those that do less live with those consequences.

My goal in life is to make my ancestors smile and know I hear and feel their energy daily. I want to respect their struggles and dreams for me by being less fearful each day. I am my ancestors' wildest dreams alive in human form. Watch me work. (And I did finally buy a house).

MY FRIEND OBI

One of the people that reflected back to me how much racism and self-applied prejudice was draining my own super powers was Obi, a friend of mine I met during undergraduate college. Obi is from Nigeria. Obi is from oil money. Let me be clear. She was from real money. For example, her father used to wire her tuition money every quarter. He got so irritated with having to stop during a business trip to wire her money he told her to go to the school's administration and ask how much her tuition would be for the next four years so he could go ahead and pay for it all at one time. Yeah. That type of money.

But she was very down to earth. We would have conversations about race and culture and compare how African Americans were different from people born in Africa. Two moments while we where hanging out will always stand out to me because they both changed my life.

The first was when I went shopping with her at an upper scale mall in La Jolla, California. For me, this was a mall Blacks never go to. It was like an unwritten social rule. WE didn't go there because we couldn't afford anything and were not welcome. But this mall was located down the street from my college so it became the only place to eat off campus or shop.

One day Obi wanted to go into this jewelry store at the La Jolla mall, and I immediately felt uncomfortable, **like I had stolen something before I even entered the store.** Obi looked at me strangely and just walked in. In the store, I noticed the customers and staff there staring at us but not offering help. Obi politely asked for help with an item on inside the glass display. She looked at in no rush. All the while, I just wanted to leave before the cops where called for shopping while Black.

When we left the store, Obi asked why I was freaking out. I explained the social history and how rude I thought they were being because we where Black. Obi was quiet for a moment and then said, **"Malik, they are at work and their job is to answer my questions and do what I ask so why would I ever care what they thought of me?"**

Life changed forever.

The second time that stood out with her was when she asked me, "Malik, why did they take you from us?" She was referring to the African Slave Trade. It was the first time I ever felt connected to Africa and disconnected at the same time. And to her question... **I still don't have an answer.**

NON-ACCREDITED NINJA

Many Black women I know complain there are no good Black men.

As I've aged, I now challenge this craziness every chance I get. **There are plenty of good Black men!!** Plenty! Sadly, a lot of Black women I've met want the good guy to also be a biker who works construction for a living and walks around with no shirt on to show off his muscles. Those two don't often come together.

I've seen what I consider good potential mates for Black woman get shot down at the door. When I ask these women what their reasons are, they reply, "He's not my type" or "He seems soft." What I've learned is a lot of these women don't even know what they want and end up tearing down a lot of good men along the way. And then when they get older, these women still look for non-accredited ninjas!! They refuse to look in the mirror and say, **"Maybe it's me."**

I know several Black women who are now single mothers who thought they could make it work with a man, who from the beginning was never into her. I know women who I've personally seen around men who worship them and would be great husbands, dismantle those men and give their hearts to men who call them when they only need money or want sex. This has become such a consistent a pattern that now my wife has started to say, **"Dang, baby, I used to be just like that,"** which supports my position that it's often a belief system these women have and a societal system that allows them to have it so they leave the blame at the feet of Black men.

I'm here to tell young brothers: Don't by that hype! If a woman ever tells you "You're ugly," "You're weak," "You're a nerd," or "You're not my type," **please take** those as red flags and run as fast as you can away from them! This is not the woman for you! MOVE ON! (And by the way I have been told all those things).

PERMISSION

The hardest thing to learn is how and when to trust your own thoughts over those around you. We all have an internal voice that guides our emotions and decision making.

What happened to me early in life is that I was taught to not trust that voice. How was this done? By being called "dumb," "stupid," "weird," and a "nerd." This constant barrage took its toll. All the way into adulthood I never took a step that had my full confidence in it.

The world offers a lot of opportunity to doubt yourself and few to develop self-confidence. Developing confidence is a different process for each individual. One area I always look to for inspiration and also as a barometer for where

I'm at with my own self confidence is stardom: athletes and rappers. Both of those occupations are filled with what some would say are over-confident people. For me, they let me listen to how they think, what they did to become successful, and what the do to remain so. I listen to their challenges and how they overcame them. I also pay attention to who they listened to and most importantly **who they ignored.** How did they face challenges? How do they handle success?

One of my favorite athletes to listen to is Shannon Sharpe. He grew up in the sticks of Georgia. Poor. He went to an historically black college, has a heavy southern accent, and was drafted in the late rounds of the NFL Draft. At each step, he has had major setbacks and acceptable excuses to give up. Yet, **each time he found a reason and a way to keep going.** At the core, he always had one thing: CONFIDENCE.

But developing confidence is not easy. I believe we all start off with a level of confidence then our environment dictates how it's fed. I think sometimes kids are teased as part of bonding. But in my life, I started at such a negative level when it came to my self-confidence that I always internalized the teasing and believed it to be true.

Confidence, to me, is allowing yourself to believe what you're telling yourself before you have any evidence. That's hard to do! Even now, I don't always know what I'm doing. What's different for my life now is that I always believe **I know longer need a guarantee.**

I've been called arrogant, and I understand why. To those on the outside, I'm truly walking my own path and it looks like I'm ignoring them or leaving them out. And sometimes I am! But what they are missing is my reasoning. For me, if you haven't done it, then most likely you ain't gonna do it! So WHY would I seek your advice? My analysis of those that have negative views of me is that they are disappointed in their own life and choices and look for comfort in seeing others develop that same fear. Well, that won't be me.

Just the other day my wife said, "You really got some odd ways." Yes, it stung because her words matter to me. But I smiled and didn't respond. Why? Because even my wife has fears and anxieties that she deals with sometimes by throwing them on me. I just looked inside myself. I looked at the big ole truck I bought for her and said to myself, "Odd pays really well." That is confidence. Even when those closest to you provide opportunities to have doubts, you can gather yourself internally and still be connected to them without anger and without losing your direction.

By the way, I think my wife is odd as heck!

REAL IS RARE

One thing I've always been is real. Now please allow me to explain. Many people over use that term and often use it as an excuse to be rude and then justifying it by saying, "I was just keeping it real." To me, being real means I don't hide my pain or emotions to look strong. This often leads to me being called "sensitive." **To that I say, thank God I'm sensitive!** It is the source of my strength. Me being aware of my emotions has allowed me to connect with others on levels and depths many will never get close to experiencing.

I often wonder where the concept of a Black man being emotionally aware simultaneously made him weak and a poor mate. I was often asked by women if I was gay because of my ability to talk about my feelings. It seemed to a lot of women that the two could not exist in a straight Black man. I do now accept that I also was sensitive in response to not knowing how to manage my seething anger. Instead of being angry, I think I elected to be docile, which seems to be more socially acceptable for young Black boys.

I have learned that enjoying being alone as a child developed me into a strong introvert. Sometimes this is a positive thing, and at other times it's a negative. I think inside I just didn't believe my presence had value so I only felt safe when I was alone. I always immediately felt intimidated around other males. I never knew how to "bag" back (share insults for humor). My insecurities wouldn't allow me to see the jokes about me as both true and also funny and okay. I always internalized the jokes and added them to my storage pile of insecurities.

I remember one time when I was living with my girlfriend at the time and she got fed up with me going into the bedroom whenever she had guest over. Hey, I was just scared of new people, and she tended to have girlfriends who had boyfriends who where gangsters. Yes. This is a true story.

So, one Saturday night, her friends came over, and I immediately **ran** to the bedroom for the night. Well, she came into the room and asked me if I was coming out to meet them. I replied, "No." She walked farther into the room and closed the door behind her. Then, she said, "This is your house, and if you are going to let another man come into your home and run you into your bedroom then you need to stay your mutha fucking ass in here!" Then she calmly walked out of the room, closing the door behind her.

Bam! I had to make some life choices in a heartbeat. Either I stay in the room and be a certified bitch in my girlfriend's eyes or face my fears and go out into the living room and meet her friends. Well, I chose the latter. I went into the living room and introduced myself. And man, this guy in the living room with his girlfriend was a full out blood. Dressed in red from head to toe, built like Debo from the movie "Friday," and had cornrows to seal the deal. Well, I grabbed my balls and got into the mix. By the time the night was over, the guy had such a good time with talking with me, before he left my house at 3 am, he said, "Blood, you fucking cool! Forget these bitches. I'm coming to kick it with you next time!

"REAL NINJAS

I'm just trying to say what's on every real Ninja's mind. Simply put: **I be scared.** A lot!! **I just be looking tough. Acting tough.** But inside sometimes, I'm shaking like a leaf. And what's real is that it's okay.

God promised me I will survive not matter what he makes me go through. He didn't say I wouldn't be scared during the process. It's the process that shakes us up. It wakes us. It makes us listen with the ears of a tiger on the hunt. It makes us focus in ways we may not have thought possible.

Real Ninjas know how to front. But real Ninjas also know that fear is just a part of life. The strong just learn how to walk with the fear. Some even learn to let it motivate them. That's where the term comes from: "Real recognizes real." Real Ninjas see the tiger in the eyes of other real Ninjas. And the tiger looks different (lawyers, doctors, basketball players), but it feels the same no matter the form it takes.

Man, sometimes I laugh at how I'm perceived. And sometimes I laugh at how little I receive my own power. Strength isn't from not being affected by things (that's called being numb). Strength comes from feeling everything, deciding what's important, and then proceeding even when you're afraid. Ain't nothing coming to you on your path you won't being able to face, overcome, and learn from.

RENAISSANCE MAN

What does it mean to be a man that is already what the world is catching up to? What does it mean to be that and also be a Black Man?

It's a Renaissance Man. He is a free thinker, unique even to himself. In the African American culture, he is often mislabeled as "weird" or a "nerd." He talks in the King's English and struggles to speak slang. In his youth, he may not be able to fit in with guys or girls. To guys, he's too soft and to girls he's too feminine.

A popular term I heard in my youth used to degrade me was "sensitive." This term is still tossed at me today as an adult, but my reaction now is a thousand percent different, both internally and externally. Internally, it used to send me into myself where I would hide. It immediately paralyzed me mentally, even though I would just smile and grin. Now I respond with specific wording, "Your inability to see my fullness is reflective of your limited development, not mine." This often stuns the person or people who called me that word, but it also creates immediate respect and sends a very clear message: "I'm not to be played with."

As a Renaissance Man, the world is often catching up to thoughts and realizations I had decades ago. It also means I'll most likely never be in alignment with the masses. What I now understand as an adult is this is always the path that the bold, strong, and free will always have to take. The Renaissance Man has to learn this in order to truly fly. He has to get comfortable with risk. He has to get comfortable with calming his own fears because the world will not understand him or his goals.

The Renaissance Man has to see peace as an internal goal. The Renaissance Man has to understand the he will always be creating his own reality and by no means can he try to make the crowd accept him because this process will only create feelings of depression. The Renaissance Man was made to create a path where others only see a wall. He is designed to make the impossible look easy.

Most importantly, the Renaissance Man was created to have a direct line with his connection with God. As long as he trusts that relationship, he will live in heaven every day while others feel they are in hell.

RULES ARE FOR POOR PEOPLE

A wise Black man once said this to me: "Rules are for poor people". I always thought it was a statement about the amount of money you had in the bank. Now that I've had money, I realized I misunderstood.

He was referring to a person's thinking. If you think poor, then, guess what, you will be poor. That's why when poor people hit the lottery, they end up poor again. Why? Because they never changed their thinking. The free thinkers are always going to be the inventors and risk takers. Rules provide the **illusion** of safety and predictability.

Case in point: My mom always encouraged me to get a full-time job. Even while I was completing my Ph.D., she always got excited about the full-time jobs I would be able to get. To me, her thinking was always crazy and Old School. I was going to school to NOT have to work for anyone! Working **with** someone vs. **for** someone are two totally separate things. Even when I completed school, my mother and I would always debate this.

Now, I'm by no means suggesting my mother has a poverty mentality. As a matter of fact, I learned about money and saving from my mother who owns real estate across the country and has several nest eggs I've had to borrow from.... with my educated self. What I do wonder is how much more my mother would have dominated if she didn't need the rules.

Don't be afraid to have a thought that the crowd disagrees with. I remember people trying to talk me out of getting my doctorate. But in my mind, I was already rich and, trust me, this was not the same for my pockets. I have written many checks that I knew where gonna bounce to the sky.

But my goals where never about money. They were about options. I wanted the options to live, travel, and smile. But that wouldn't happen on a clock decided by a person or company.

Rules can keep your creativity at bay so it never reaches its potential. Think of even Jesus. They literally tried to kill him, but he was rich in mind, body, and soul. He was so rich he gave to the mentally poor while they hated him the whole time.

As you move through life, look for opportunities to free yourself from any thoughts of poverty that may be holding you back versus setting you spiritually and emotionally free to do what God put you here to do.

STEAKS

During my medical psychology internship at Duke University Medical Center, I was mentored by Dr. Christopher Edwards. As he and I got closer, I began to talk more deeply with him about my fears, insecurities, and problems in relationships. We talked about everything. We especially connected on our love for cooking. I later compared his cooking to me being a short order cook at a greasy spoon and him being a Michelle 5-star Chef.

One day after internship, he asked me if I wanted to follow him to Sam's Club and use that time to talk about the day's events. (That would eventually become our check-in time with each other, and, boy. did I love it). While he shopped, I blabbed on. I complained about

145

internship. About how hard it was. How bad I was being treated. **You know, the normal stuff powerless people complain about instead of taking advantage of those challenges.**

He would just listen. He never judged. Sometimes, he'd offer reframes or alternative views. At other times, he would just be empathetic and agree, which helped me a lot because I felt validated. Ultimately, it helped me be more open to his suggestions for change.

While we talked, he filled up his cart, throwing in toilet paper, juice, chips, candies, sodas (pops, soft drinks), milk, bread, basically whatever he put his eyes on. Finally, he would throw in the steaks. He showed me the steaks each time, explain the different types, cuts, and flavors. He also showed me how to select the better cuts based on the marbling. It was always a lesson.

I'm looking at the steaks and his cart and thinking, "Wow, you can afford all that?" Let me be clear his cart was overflowing. I never saw anyone shop like that. I normally got three items, and I'm out. That was eye-opening. After paying for the items I walked to his truck to help him unload, at this point he asked me to hold like half the stuff that was in the cart. I'm cool. Anything to help and spend more time together.

After he loads his truck up, he says, "All the stuff in your arms is for you!" Wow! Man! He gave me juice, toilet paper, a bag of large russet baking potatoes, whole garlic cloves, A1 sauce, and a bunch of other items—and some rib eye steaks. Before leaving, he added, **"I eat, you eat; I'll text you later a recipe to make the steaks with."**

Man! And so my introduction to steaks had just occurred. Here I was a broke graduate student, starving but had a freezer full of steaks marinating. It was one of those life events I'll never forget. And he texted me the recipe!

I'm sure it would have tasted great, but I had NO idea how to make steaks so I ended up burning them up and smoking my house up for a week. But later on, Dr. Edwards came over and showed me how to cook them to perfection. I still burnt a few after that. Even then he told me, "That's the only way you gonna learn is by making a few mistakes and learning from them." I love that man!

STOP PRETENDING

Stop Pretending To Be Small!!

It doesn't serve you, and it disrespect the gifts God blessed you with!

In the African American community when you become successful, it's treated like a surprise versus what's supposed to happen in your life. This breeds a feeling of isolation and anxiety. It has made me feel like I have no one to share my experiences with. It makes me anxious because I live with a constant fear that with one bad step it will all end.

What has helped is finding those who are where I want to be. And that's not limited to only African Americans. I have been able to gain insights from people of all colors and genders because I stopped pretending that I knew it all and starting asking for guidance.

I grew up with the heart of a pit bull, but I would pretend I was a poodle. I was often the smartest in the room, but I had been hiding it to belong. **I feared being seen**. Made fun of. What's sad is no matter all of those attempts to hide, I was still made fun of and called names.

What was amazing was as I learned to stand up for myself, I noticed others started to sit down and shut up! My mom told me once, "They gonna talk about you anyway so DO YOU!"

Stop hiding from your best self. Do what comes from inside. And for God's, sake stop pretending!

STUPID FAITH

The best way to know you're on your path is when those who haven't gone before you are trying to talk you out of it!

I remember so clearly in 1997 when I started to share with others my dream of getting my Ph.D. in Psychology. I recall an older African American male telling me, "It's too many people with Ph.D.'s. You should just get a Masters." (Mind you, HE had a Ph.D.!) I remember another time someone just laughed in my face. To that person I wasn't good enough or of high enough caliber to dream that high.

I look back and see it was THEIR own self-doubts and limited dreams they where projecting on to me. Fortunately, I'm so retarded I didn't listen. **Instead, I got**

angry and got motivated. The best way to motivate me back then (and sometimes now) is to tell me I can't do something. It immediately shifts me into a "Screw you!" mentality, and I go to work in silence. And that's just what I did. I grinded and hustled until I got into an APA approved Ph.D. program in Clinical Psychology! **Middle finger to all the haters! Thanks for the motivation.**

Heavy is the Head that Wears the Crown

TALENT WILL SHOW UP WITH DETERMINATION

Recently, a good friend of mine and I were talking about her career plans, and I suggested she pursue her doctorate, given she has completed two master's degrees and wanted to continue her education. Her response was, "I'm not ready for all that."

Her response hurt me. It hurt because I hated to feel she was doubting herself after all she has accomplished. It was listening to her set a limit on her abilities that left me wounded. Wounded because after all the years of knowing her, I couldn't help her. This was and is a moment she has to face herself.

It's hard for me because in my life even now I know so many people who put invisible limits on themselves. Even my mother does it. My sister has two master's degrees and is finishing her doctorate as I complete this book, and yet my mother doubts her own abilities to pursue education. She says, "That's for you all, not me." But I've been around the "smart" people in academia and also in business, and let me tell you, my mom runs circles around them in both worlds. But even my mom has her own hurdles.

What I've learned is that to be successful you literally just have to jump and develop the tools and wings you need on the way down. **This is truly trusting God.** But I see many people don't know how to take these leaps of faith. I know from my own life that the tools I have needed will always present themselves when I needed them but never before.

Oftentimes in life, there is no "get ready." The dreams you may have will only come true once you start the journey. The process builds you, not the delay. **The delay**

only promotes fears. To quote the great CeeLo Green of the Goodie Mob, "Get up, get out, and get something; don't let the days of your life pass you by."

THE BOYS ARE TO BE PROTECTED

B lack boys are to be protected. Have you ever heard anyone say this? I haven't. But at my core, I now it's true.

Protecting doesn't mean shielding. It does mean loving. It does mean letting them know they have value to the world. It means really showing them throughout history they have had a place. A role. A voice.

I grew up not feeling I had any history. Not feeling I came from any place in the universe. To the many, Barack Obama seemed to have changed the worldview of African Americans. But for me, the movie *Black Panther* changed the worldview in the hearts of Black people. *Blank Panther* presented a perfect model of Black thought, a balance between historic legacy and a dominate foothold in the modern world. No niggas. No sluts. No fake gangstas. Just pure Black excellence.

At the end of the movie came the most powerful visual when the young Black boy didn't follow the crowd to the revealed spaceship. Instead he was drawn to the Black male energy. And he asked the best question of a young mind ever: "Who are you?"

Who are you? Not what have you been told you are, but in your private moments, who are you?

The Black boys are to be protected. Are you protecting you? Are you going to school daily? Are your daily actions moving you toward your goals? Have you set goals? How are you measuring them? Do your goals add to the lives of your community? Is faith part of your goals?

The first part of protecting the Black boys is protecting their thoughts and dreams. Don't let them be limited.

Don't make them feel bad for speaking "proper English" or not wanting to play sports. Protect the Black boys from the judgments of those with limited dreams because any Black boy with big dreams will always scare the adults around them. Black boys are so invisible to the world that they sadly become invisible to us. They are our greatest treasures. **Our breathing gold.**

Protect Black boys, and you change the world.

THE CONSTANT MONSTER

Worry (the clinical definition is uncontrollable ruminations) is the Constant Monster in my life. It wakes me up in the morning and sometimes keeps me up at night. I believe many men choose to do nothing in life and lean on drugs to manage the worry and try to keep it asleep. Worry makes the mind drift like a piece of driftwood in an ocean storm. Worry makes the possible seem impossible, and, to make matters worse, it feeds on itself and makes more worries. My Grandfather used to say: "Worry is like a rocking chair. It makes you feel like your moving but you ain't going nowhere."

I also believe the use of marijuana by a lot of African American males is to manage this constant mental stress and micro-aggressions. I believe it's become socially acceptable to smoke marijuana, but the "why" isn't often explored. Why do so many people "need" to escape daily? What is it about life that's so overwhelming that many people just can't cope without some type of self-medication, whether it be prescribed or self-administered? To be clear, I place know value judgment either way. I believe whatever gets you through your day is up to you, as long as it doesn't hurt someone else to do it.

THE CORE OF WHITE PRIVILEGE

The core of White privilege is expectation. White people, more specifically, White men expect to win! **Black people EXPECT to lose!** Instead of tapping into our ancestral roots and unlimited super powers, we look for better ways to lesson our losses instead of expanding our ability to gain.

Try exploring the magic of expecting success. I mean truly work at every goal you have with the true belief everything in the universe is working with you! That's where the old saying comes from "Everyone gets behind a winner." Winners win because they do a few specific things. First, they put in the work. Next, they believe. Third, they ignore noise. And finally, they stop looking for people to agree with them and learn to agree with themselves!

When I read interviews by Puff Daddy, Jay Z, Bill Gates, and Scarface (the rapper), they all have a drive that comes from within to be the best at their craft and they never listen to the crowd. The crowd is made up of folks who never have and never will do anything new. **The crowd expects failure and handouts.**

Work on your cognitions. You control your thoughts, only you. This was something I had to learn. Wake each morning and say, **"What are God and I going to accomplish today?"**

Take the time during your day to pray. Pray for the confidence to take leaps when fear arises. Pray for the faith that your words will come from the purist parts of you. Know that God hears you before you even speak. Your thoughts will become your reality. Whatever you think you are becomes the truth! Your truth.

Winners except that the journey will sometimes feel lonely, but they know God is always with them. He didn't create any of us to fail! He created you to blaze your own path. Expect success. Expect your abilities will carry you, and your internal magnet will draw the people and tools you need to attain anything. And I literally mean anything!

THE DISCONNECTED

The disconnected can leave their children and never look back. In extreme cases like my own, the disconnected will leave themselves also (mine committed suicide). It has led me to feel suicidal throughout my life when I felt overwhelmed and alone (a deadly combination). For this reason, choosing a life partner is critical. For a Black man, his home has to feel safe and supportive. This may also be why some Black men marry outside our culture due to the historic conflicts between Black men and Black women. Unfortunately, it is the healing between Black man and Black woman that is needed to help provide the foundation many Black men are in life-threatening need of and don't know it.

THE FATHERLESS KING

Like Moses, I was raised by men who will never be my father. From them, I have gained strengths and ways of a king that, had my father lived, I may never have learned.

I'm a king. But one without a father. There are many like me, but I'm of the blessed class. I'm blessed that the men who did contribute in my development were men of the highest quality, and, more specifically, they were all men of faith in God. Kings are at their best when they know they have limits and are guided by a power even greater than themselves.

I'm a fatherless king, but still a king. There are many little princes growing up without a father. And they don't even know they are kings. They don't know their own greatness is as close as their last breath because they don't have anyone to tell them.

I'm saying to all fatherless kings like myself: **YOU HAVE VALUE**. Get on your throne and never leave it.

THE GAP

My friend Carl was my hero for years. He never really knew it until years later. And, honestly, neither did I.

I met Carl through a mutual friend who was attending University of California, San Diego with him. For me, he was the first African American male I met in my age group who was not into gang banging and really valued the pursuit of higher education. At the time, I met Carl I was flunking out of community college(s), was a teen parent, and still living at home with my mom. So, to me, he was immediately a new and possible standard. He was smart, funny, and confident, but not a briefcase carrying nerd as I was told I was often throughout my life.

Carl was a balance I hadn't seen. He was cool. He was articulate. But he was also down to earth and very smart. Several years later when I was living in Atlanta, I reconnected with Carl who was also living there. We were out eating lunch one day, and he made a comment that left me feeling judged. It was basically him saying I needed to not be so anxious around him and in life overall. I took offense. To me, I was just showing my excitement about having him as a friend, but he was looking at me like I was a stalker or unwanted groupie.

I told him, "Look you grew up with a father and from his support you grew up with a confidence I don't have. Every step you take is certain. You don't waiver or carry doubt in your decisions. For me, every step I take is filled with doubt and fear. Unlike you, I don't have much confidence so when I'm around you, I'm trying to get as much of it as I can from being in your presence." From that moment on I started living by Ice Cubes lyric "only stars I know are in sky". No more false Gods. Trust yourself.

THE HEAD NOD

I remember walking down the street with my classmate during graduate school, and as a I was passing another African American male, I nodded my head at him and kept crossing the street with my classmate. My classmate asked, "Why do you always do that?" I didn't know what he was talking about so I asked, and he replied, "Whenever you see another Black man, you nod your head at each other."

I nod because as a silent way of communicating to them "I see you". "I recognize you". "You are not invisible to me" and depending on the neighborhood it also means "This is not a hostile encounter unless you want it to be one."

The head nod also ask the question friend or foe (which one are you?). It's like two warriors meeting on a path. The head nod settles the issue of respect and acceptance.

If the other person doesn't nod back at me that's a signal that I need to be on alert.

Sometimes, it means I ain't no punk and I'm not afraid to engage you based on your response (or non-response)

It comes down to reducing the feeling of invisibility. But it also says I'm down for me and mine if the shit pops off.

THE HOLE INSIDE

Today, I mis my dad. Tomorrow, I will mis him even more. This will continue for the rest of my life. Why? Because as I grow and now watch my children grow, I see where I fit in their lives and where my father's suicide created holes inside mine. I will always feel like I'm guessing if I'm doing the right things with my life. I will never be able to ask my father for advice. I will never be able to spend time with him, talking about challenges only he could understand.

The hole inside feels like it gets bigger each day, and I'd be lying if I didn't admit that it hurts. It hurts because my sons will never get to know him, and he will never get to know them. I feel adrift as a man, and I feel this could have been prevented. I know I'm not the only Black boy that wishes his dad was around. I'm just trying to add words to the feelings we have to live with daily.

Dads are anchors in the storms of life for their children. Boys need there's. Dads show them how to be men, not grown boys. Boys need their dads to talk to them and show them love and confidence. Today, many men are just grown boys, pretending they know what they are doing. They don't have a clue! I think sometimes acknowledging this pain is too much for the boys who feel alone. So, they bottle it up and become angry men, then angry husbands, and eventually angry fathers.

Your father's journey is not yours. You can change the generations that follow you if you connect to the love inside you and teach your boys how to have that same love for themselves.

THE HUNGER

L ooking back, I have always been driven and self-motivated. Often, this was due to not wanting to go through the hassle of asking my mother for any type of money. It just always felt like begging. I'm a strong believer that some people have to make it cost you (even if it's an emotional cost) before giving or doing something for you. And I just decided early on that asking my mom for anything **cost too damn much emotionally.** She will laugh to this day and say, "I know you hate asking me for anything!" Man, the first time she said that to me I felt betrayed. It was like she knew all along.

As I live now, I try to find the balance between giving my kids the world while also not robbing them of the opportunity to learn how to go get it for themselves but also comfortable asking for what they NEED (vs. Want).

THE "L" IS IN YOUR HEAD

Who are you really scared of? Who or whatever it is doesn't exist outside of your head! The fear is irrational. The boogie man is not coming to get you. You're creating your losses. You can learn how to create only victories. The only difference between a poor person and a millionaire is self-doubt. The poor person has tons of it, and the millionaire has no idea what it is.

The "L" (lose) is all created in your head and plays out in your life. Life is truly too short to be afraid of anything or anyone. The second you're afraid, it's just like giving up. Fear only paralyzes, it is not designed to motivate. Being cautious is not bad. **Paralysis over what CAN happen is deadly**. The "L" Is ONLY In Your head!

THE LOUDEST VOICE

Growing up, I believe I was taught to listen to the opinions and values of others and unconsciously ignore my own. Over time, I believe I learned to silence my inner voice so much I never knew what I actually thought. And when I explored my own wishes, I felt I was being selfish. I see now that most successful people are secretly selfish.

For me, I had to redefine selfishness. To me it now means, I'm operating within God's plan when I'm listening to myself and what my goals are. God didn't place any of us here to listen to others to the point of ignoring what He placed inside us. I believe oftentimes depression is created from the ignoring of our own desires and wishes.

Does that mean I ignore others? Not at all. It just means I'm selective with whom I seek counsel, and, even still, I never surrender my own permission to change my mind. You have to be careful when receiving advice, especially from people who give advice with the unannounced expectations you will do as they say.

Your voice has to always be the Loudest Voice inside. We all share a reality. But we do not have to submit to a belief that someone else's reality is THE reality we all have to submit to.

THE SCARIEST THING

The scariest thing in life is the moment you realize your parents are human and can't give you the advice you need to get you through something. I mean it's scary as hell to be going through a life event and your parents just don't have the words to sooth your fears. Even when they try, you know your heart still needs something more. It can make you feel alone. In these moments, I've learned to thank my mom for all the years she could help me in those moment---and then grab my balls and pray!!

THE TOP OF THE HILL IS JUST A STATE OF MIND

You can think you're at the bottom and be looking down from the top of the hill and never know it. It is truly a state of mind.

I grew up middle class. I never felt poor. I never felt the need to feel bad about not growing up "rough" or "hard." African-Americans (especially males) like to judge each other on how and where we grew up. The rougher the neighborhood, the stronger and tougher you are believed to be. Made of more grit. I call bullshit!

In my eyes, it easy to stay in the neighborhood you grew up in. Live in your momma's house (even after she dies) and sell drugs. It takes more heart and fight to travel, go to colleges that are predominately not Black, and find a way!

Find a way to keep your cultural roots. This will keep you mentally focused when nothing around you reinforces your sense of self. Believe in your dreams even when you return home to your community you went to school to help and they then label you a "sell-out." That's a real thug to me.

Being on the top of the hill in your mind and soul allows you to be in alignment internally. It allows you to hear your voice above all others. You might think others are happier, have more money, more women, etc. But they can all still be at the bottom of the hill looking up to you.

Being at the top of the hill doesn't mean you have to feel better than others either. What it means is your goals are your own and you have peace inside and not disruption when you're around others who may not be able to understand the directions your paths are taking you. Move out of the "either/or" thinking. Move to the "all of the above" mentality.

African-Americans sometimes believe we have to be either cool or a nerd ("either/or" mentality). I have decided I can be both and more than that if it decide I want to be something else. A label someone else puts on you can become a definition of your life. YOU be your own scribe and write your story as YOU see fit. No rules unless you make them. No limits ever. And, of course, develop the ability to expect the fall and know the growth is in your ability to know that learning happens as you learn to get back up. **Still standing, always standing.**

THE FATHER VS THE SON

One of my closest friends talks to me about his relationship with his father and how often its negative. Or as my friend says, "It's a room filled with things unsaid."

Growing up without my father has made me hyper-sensitive to Black father and son relationships so I always encourage my friend to speak to his father about his feelings of anger and disappointment about a lot of the things his father did and said when my friend was a child. Let me give some context. My friend is younger than I am, but he is someone I look up to and call for counsel and support. So, for him to not face this challenge, let's me know how delicate it is for him and how painful the memories are.

One thing for sure is we all become the parents of our parents. What I mean is at some point when you become an adult, you will start to challenge your parents' advice and question decisions they made during your childhood that you as an adult with children don't think made any sense.

My friend had to deal with his father's infidelity when he was in his teens and he was the one that unfortunately discovered his father's cheating and had to make a grown-up decision as a child. He had to decide if he was going to live with his father's lie or tell his mother and devastate her life. From what I understand, my friend never told his mother, but she did find out. This event, combined with others, created a chasm between him and his father that neither has repaired.

Now that my friend is married and has his own family, he finds himself conflicted when he speaks with his dad about anything. I believe this comes from my friend's faith in God and his innate desire to live in the light and feel congruence with the truth no matter how painful it is. My friend's father is a very confident man who runs his own businesses. Where they have the biggest challenge is my friend's father needing and wanting a closer relationship with his son whom he is beyond proud of. Due to his own issues, he doesn't know how to build that relationship. Instead, his father asks my friend for help is getting his businesses to become more modern and productive financially. My friend has tried and tried to help his father, but his father is so afraid to show weakness that it ruins any attempt at support through my friend's offers.

What I see in my friend's father I see often in fragile men. The father wants a relationship with the son but only on his terms. And those terms always have inside of them the requirement that the son cannot be the leader. This insecurity on the part of the father keeps the maladaptive communication patterns going while simultaneously blocking any room for real growth and new ways of being between father and son. It's the perfect set up because it leaves all the burden on the son to make all the changes and the father can pick and choose like he's at a salad bar.

I recommended to my friend that he has to take the role of father to his own dad. He will have to have what is called a "coming to Jesus" conversation with him. My friend has to be uncomfortable enough inside to say what his father did that hurt him as a child and what is hurting him now as an adult. For my friend, I know this is hard. I mean who wants to challenge their Dad's love? However, I believe what my friend's dad says is irrelevant. I believe the real opportunity is for my friend. It's an opportunity for him to show himself to himself. He can show he's different from his own father by being bold enough to have the hard conversation unlike his father who has never been able to do that unless he set the rules in advance.

THE YOUNGER YOU

I often ask myself what I would tell the younger me if I could go back and share insights on how to manage what's coming.

The first thing I would tell the younger me is to not worry so much. I look back and see decades of depression that was brought on by needless worrying. I worried as a way to feel some sense of control in times when I felt I had no direction for my life. Worry takes over a creative mind. Worry also waste creative energy by using thought energy generating scenarios and outcomes that will NEVER happen. The worrying also released chemicals my body that increased my depressive thoughts that had a trickle-down effect on my relationships, moods, daily activities, and my overall hope for a positive future.

I would tell the younger me that I'm strong. I don't remember ever being told that. I don't remember being told my being smart was a good thing. I didn't know it's the smart people that run the world. I wish I had known there were other Black males who would accept me and not make me feel alone.

I would hug me and spend time with me asking me about my thoughts. I would ask me about girls. What type of girls I liked? What did I plan to do in life? I would ask me about how do I set goals (I didn't have any, other than getting a girlfriend). I would talk to me about what to tell myself when I felt scared and hopeless. I would tell me that worrying is like a rocking chair, it makes you feel like your moving but your really in the same place. I would tell myself to smile more and enjoy the silence.

I would tell myself to look at all the people in my life and know they all see something great in me and my job is to find it.

THINGS BLACK MEN AREN'T ALLOWED TO TELL THEMSELVES

(What White men already know but Black men need to re-learn)

Black men need to learn they can do anything. I mean that literally. During a long conversation with two other black men, it hit me that there are core truths about my identity that have gone underdeveloped. Part of this comes from what I believe is what Black men are not allowed or taught to NOT tell ourselves that White men get reminded of daily.

We don't tell ourselves we can be of value to the world.

We are not allowed to believe we are loving and caring by nature.

We are not shown we are loved and can be sensitive.

We are not told we are lovable.

We are not made to believe we can be successful.

White men live in a world where they don't even have to question their worth or value!

Black men have to really start to ask themselves not only what they think but also what they feel. We need to develop a consistent voice inside that is always the first voice we listen to.

While talking to my brothers, I often hear talk about situations they faced that were similar to challenges I've experienced but in totally different ways than I did. And often what I sense is they felt a sense of control of the moment and the mental and emotional strength to guide the outcome. For me, I always felt like I was a victim to the outcome and would have to deal with the repercussions of the negative outcomes.

This is what made me look up to other Black men and what makes me still believe that this is what young Black boys are looking for when they join gangs. It's what I think women that like bad boys are attracted to. I believe they are seeking men who project control and confidence of their lives and its many destinations.

What I've learned is this is often an illusion and many of these brothas are just as insecure as the next. That's not to say I haven't met real gangstas. But inside each of the men I looked up to was an internal strength that was self-guided, self-validated. No matter what the outside force was, they where always able to trust the voice inside to guide them. As Black men, the more we each practice affirming our own life as valuable and essential to the growth of our families, the more we will see the trends and outcomes of our community change in ways that immediately become more in alignment with those of our ancestors.

TIPTOEING WHEN I SHOULD BE STOMPING

You can be to loving to a person when you are so paralyzed by the fear of them not loving you or being angry at you. It will ultimately lead to you losing your boundaries to the point they don't exist. Tiptoeing is knowing the person is talking to you like your dirt with a smile and calling it love and you don't call them on it. Tiptoeing is when you continue to allow this to happen, hoping the person sees you're a good person inside and on their own will start treating you better, just like you treat them.

Nope. It will never happen.

The only way to get what you need out of any relationship is to always know **you have to teach people**

how to treat you. It means knowing **your God's child,** and He didn't put you on earth to be walked on. Not loved. Not valued.

It's time to start stomping. Stomping is stopping people the moment you feel slighted and point out with the correction you need: "Don't speak to me like that." or "I won't allow you to disrespect me." And be prepared for people to call YOU sensitive **(understand that's just a distraction technique by them).** Stay on message and keep your foot on their neck. When you're defending your feelings and teaching someone how to treat you, if you have your foot on their neck emotionally, **always press harder.**

Folks will then have to decide to love you by your expectations or move on. Either way you win. Those that value your presence will always adapt, and those that want to use you will leave.

Stop tiptoeing with your truth and start stomping!!

TOE-TO-TOE

Can you go toe-to-toe with your fears? Can you know inside at your core you are afraid but at the same time give yourself no option to run? Can you accept that the only praise you need has to come from within? Can you wake up every morning and ask yourself what are the 5 things that scare you the most and then make a list of the 4 things you will do that day to knock them down? Can you ignore the crowd and listen to your voice? Do you believe that if you think you can, you can? Can you leave those behind that can't run with you? Can you accept being alone is sometimes part of the journey? Can you believe that God believes you can do all these things?

I do.

WATCH WHAT YOU FEED.
IT TENDS TO GROW

Watch what you feed. What you allow into your mind will grow if you let it. Just because someone is a close, caring friend doesn't mean you have to always accept their advice. Develop and learn to trust your own filter and advice.

I've learned that most people give advice based on the mood and moment they themselves are living in. So, if they are in a good space, then the advice they share will come from that soil. If they are in a negative space, the words they produce will come from that soil.

Speak life into everything you do. It doesn't have to be a loud formal proclamation. It can be as subtle as a soft whisper to yourself, "I can do this."

Words are powerful. And so is doubt. Most successful people teach themselves to turn the volume up on their own positive thoughts and turn the volume down on doubt. This does not mean they never have doubts or insecurities. It simply means they aren't paralyzed by them when they come up.

WHAT'S THE SECRET
TO MY SUCCESS?

The secret to my success is learning to not be afraid of my genius.

I've noticed a lot of African Americans males on some unconscious level are intimidated or even afraid of very smart African Americans. This fear leads to some very unique behaviors such as belittling them by calling them a "nerd" or other slurs. To be an African American male and successful, at some point you have to stop being afraid to become your own genius. A genius is comfortable being left to themselves to develop and grow how they see fit. It's hard to accept you are the smartest one in the room when all you want to do is be accepted.

I had to start asking myself if the people I wanted to be accepted by were even worthy. Often, my honest answer was no. It's hard to want to look up to the elders in my life to only be weighed down by their failures and burdens of the dreams they never pursued. Some of them are just living, waiting to die. No direction. No plans. No goals.

To be your own genius, you have to be willing to set your own rules. Accept that everyday rules are for poor people. But I don't mean financially poor. I mean mentally and emotionally poor. They have no energy or desire in their minds to be challenged. More often than not they fear being seen. To be your own genius, you have to remind yourself that no matter who is around you that you will always be striving to be your best even when you're in an empty room.

And the last thing you have to learn is not to feel you ever have to apologize for wanting to be all God tooled you to become. If another person decides to hate on you for being good at becoming you, then let them hate. Use it as motivation.

WHO ARE YOU KINDER TO?

Who are you kinder to? Others or yourself?

I have often been kinder to others, thinking their happiness would flow back onto me. It never worked. And I did this for decades.

The funny (and sad) thing about some people is the more you give the more they will take. I have learned the more I learn to say "No" or speak my truth the fewer headaches I have and the less I am holding on to stress.

I always tell people happiness costs. Happiness is not something people are. Happiness comes from being able to be guided by what makes you happy and centered, even if others hate it. Happy people are challenged daily. People will say crazy things to you like "What are you so happy for?" Or "Why you smiling?" As if it's unnatural.

That happy voice inside you is the most precious thing God allows you to keep when you leave heaven and fall to earth during birth. Protect it. Develop it.

Remember depression is anger turned inward. Never live a life where you're swallowing poison, hoping someone else dies. If you're swallowing the poison of self -induced silence, stop!! Speak your truth first to yourself and get comfortable with it. Then tell the world, and let them deal with their own feelings!

A great poet, Tupac, once said, "momma said never stop until you bust them up, fuck the world if they can't adjust, it's just as well"

WHY NOT YOU?

Why not you? If you can help spend your whole life believing the worst can and will happen, then the opposite has to be true also. **You can also believe the best and most amazing things can happen to you!**

I have to often work on my own thinking. I now ask myself that question daily when I catch myself worrying or looking for the negative. I take a deep breath. Exhale and say "okay." **Start over.** Start now thinking about how not only the positive can happen but how you expect it to happen.

I have studied many successful and happy people, and a commonality they share is the strong belief that their thoughts determine their outcomes. You ever notice how when successful people are giving a lecture on how they became successful, they all tend to have a little smile in their voice? I used to assume this was because they had the peace inside of knowing they don't have to ever worry about money again.

Now, I believe differently. I believe that smile comes from a deep internal knowing. Almost like an inside joke. It comes from a fire inside that they know can never be taken away once it's lit. That if they had to start over today, they would still be successful. Just like when Michael Jordan would slam dunk, folks would see him smile. The smile was from him knowing they couldn't stop him even if they wanted to!

You can't be stopped! The only person that can beat you is also the only person that can raise you from the ashes of your fears. That person is you! It's always been you.

So I ask. Why not you? Why can't you be the leader? The person with the original thoughts that can speak them into existence? Malcom and Martin asked themselves the same questions, and we know how they answered it, based on how they lived. Greatness is within you! It's as close as your breath. YOU just have to start believing it, and the rest will start to fall in place. I promise.

WORRYING IS A LIE

Choosing to believe in a worry is like choosing to believe in a lie. And like a lie, you have to keep telling more lies to keep it alive.

I have worried my whole life. I sometimes think of myself as a professional worrier. Olympic level. Looking at myself at this point in my life, I see I worried because I was afraid to try. What I am teaching myself daily is that **I can simply choose not to worry.** I can reprogram my mind to expect the best just like I spent years expecting the worst. Let me say it another way. We can make this journey whatever we want. But it all starts with our thoughts.

As African Americans, we start with a belief system that says the negative is always on the way. **But this can't be**

what my ancestors believed. If it was, they would have all stopped fighting and stopped praying. So along the way, our Negro spirituals and songs of hope turned into songs of doubt.

Worry is a lie. The truth is I can be anything the moment I believe and live like it's possible. Worrying occupies the mind but also takes away your ability to problem solve. The devil is a lie and worry is his best tool in the minds of my people. Fight the devil each time you question yourself.

Put simply, **all of the goals you set should feel impossible**, but that's the point. Why set a goal to do what someone else has already done? Set goals that scare you and in the process you shame the devil and praise God, while showing love and respect to your ancestors that wish they had the opportunities and freedoms you may be wasting daily.

YOU BROUGHT US HERE

When you rise, they will hee and haw and act like you just smacked them in the face. Just remind them, "You brought us here."

Some people assume when I'm being silent, I'm agreeing. **Wrong.** Sometimes I'm ignoring. Sometimes I'm just showing respect. But don't ignorantly assume I'm agreeing. Don't assume your plan or suggestions for me have become MY plans for me.

A lot of these same people will become offended the second you show them the power of having your own voice, even if it's a whisper. When you start to stand, they will respond in ways that make them the victim. When this happens simply say, "Your actions and your behaviors brought us here."

YOU GOTTA HAVE
A PLACE (AT FIRST)

You gotta have a place where you can go into yourself and slow the world down.

It's important that I learned to value silence. And silence happens differently for everyone. Some experience inner silence through meditation. For others, it's through church or religion. For me, it's through reading a good book.

To reset the mind, it has to be given a time to rest and relax. To float and dream without any demanded direction. You gotta have a place where you can feel and hear your own voice.

You know you're feeling it when it gives you a sense of calm from within. When you're in your own silent place, you will feel and know all things are possible and at the same time you will know God is in control so you should have no fear. Outside of this silent place, the world makes you think you are in control and that if things don't work out, it's your fault. Inner peace clams these thoughts and feelings. Inner silence lets you know when it's your dream or the world's dream for you.

Find and always keep a silent place to go to. Always know how to use it to restore you back to center.

EPILOGUE
GROWTH

God purges the dead branches so new and stronger branches can grow. Growth always take place in the Valley, never at the top of the Mountain!!!

CONTACT THE AUTHOR

Please feel free to contact the author, Dr. Malik Muhammad.

Website: www.mysilentloud.com

Email: mysilentloud@gmail.com

This book is available on Amazon.

Made in the USA
Middletown, DE
23 November 2019